Lunations and Predictions

Sophia Mason

ISBN: 0-86690-077-2

Fifth Printing: 2001

Published by:
American Federation of Astrologers, Inc.
PO Box 22040
6535 S. Rural Road
Tempe, AZ 85285-2040

Printed in the United States of America

Books by Sophia Mason

Forecasting With New, Full and Quarter Moons
Basic Fundamentals of the Natal Chart
Aspects Between Signs
Understanding Planetary Placements
Lunations and Predictions
The Art of Forecasting
Delineation of Progressions
From One House To Another

Contents

Lunations and
Predictions

Forecasting with the use of New and Full Moons is an ancient art which has been lost through the ages. Although many modern astrologers are fully aware of the potentials in using this method, they have not made it a practice to teach it to their students.

What is a Lunation? It is the conjunction of the Sun and Moon in the same sign and degree, and occurs every 28 days or thirteen times a year. The Full Moon occurs 14 days after the New Moon and is the opposition of the Sun and Moon. Almost any form of ephemeris lists the dates of the New and Full Moons on the top of each page. With uncanny accuracy the Lunation can predict the possibilities of events that will occur before the next month's Lunation takes place.

Very often the Full Moon brings to a head the events predicted by the New Moon, or it adds to or colors the events that were indicated by the New Moon. Because New and Full Moons occur in the same degree and sign only once every 19 years, it is of extreme importance to limit the orb of influence from the Sun and Moon to not more than five degrees from natal or progressed planets.

A 10 degree orb is allowed to transiting planets because the events will not be the same every 19 years. They will be in different signs and houses, indicating different individuals or circumstances that affecting the native's life.

The transiting planets on the day of the Lunation should be placed around the natal chart in the same degree and sign in which they appear in the ephemeris. This works like a mini-scope for the month ahead.

Basic Rules and Instructions

1. Place the "2 in 1" chart containing both natal and progressed planets in a clear plastic folder so that the Lunation's position and the transiting planets for that day can be written on the plastic (use a water-based felt pen). When the month is over, erase those planetary positions and insert the new ones.

2. Use the Lunation exactly as it appears in the ephemeris (the conjunction or opposition does not take place until the Moon reaches the Sun's sign and degree). Use an orb of five degrees to natal and progressed planets, and 10 degrees orb with transiting planets.

3. Average length of influence:

Solar Eclipse - one to two years in effect
Lunar Eclipse - six months to one year in effect
New Moon - four weeks in effect
Full Moon - two weeks in effect

4. Place the transiting planets around the natal and progressed chart in the same degree and sign in which they appear in the ephemeris on the day of the Lunation. This serves as a sort of mini-scope, giving the basic action to be expected during the ensuing month and indicating the kind of individuals or circumstances that will affect the native's affairs.

5. Use only a one degree orb of influence from transiting planets to natal or progressed planets; with a wider orb they either seem to lose their importance or the aspect does not consummate itself.

6. Progressed planets, except for the slower moving planets (Saturn, Uranus, Neptune and Pluto) are in signs and degrees different from those in the natal chart. The New and Full Moons, although usually occurring in a house different from that in the natal chart, often confirm what the natal chart is trying to say. Sometimes the natal chart does not receive significant aspects from the Lunation or transiting planets, but the progressed chart will, or vice versa. Or, there may be two entirely different indications, one from the natal and another from the progressed chart.

7. Many a trine or square from a transiting planet to the Natal or Progressed planets have gone unfelt or unnoticed by a beginning

astrologer, while others tend to leave a great impact. Why? Because it seems to take the effect of the Lunation to set them off. In other words, should transiting Venus square Natal Saturn on the day of the Lunation within the one degree allowable orb, its effect will be felt during the ensuing month. Through years of research on New and Full Moons as a means of predicting, if a transiting planet is more than 1 degree orb on the day of the Lunation, it just does not seem to register towards any type of action during the coming month. Some individuals have had transiting Uranus square their Natal Sun without any effect at all. The only answer could lie in the fact that the aspect was not exact or in 1 degree orb at the time of a Lunation, it must have taken place in between the 2 Lunations.

8. Every month will not hold an exciting event, as human lives tend to run on everyday happenings. What the Lunation will disclose is the main event for the coming month. It may be a friend trying to borrow money with no intention of paying it back. An unexpected change of plans may occur or, perhaps, problems with children at school. A wide variety of examples are included in this book - some heavy, some light - to illustrate the possibilities of what can be seen. However, where important events did occur such as suicide, death or surgery, there were progressed aspects to natal planets in effect during that time. The New Moon, Full Moon, Eclipse or progressed Moon (or a combination with both a Lunation and progressed Moon in aspect) generally had a hand in timing the events.

9. To determine when the actual event predicted by the Lunation will occur, it is imperative to watch the transiting Moon or Sun (or both) as they leave the conjunction position and transit through the natal or progressed chart. Very often one of these two will make an aspect to the planet that was activated in that chart on the day of the Lunation by another transiting planet, or it will enter the house the planet rules. By working with the Lunation and watching the transiting Moon and Sun for several months as they trigger action, the student will learn what to watch for.

10. If neither the Lunation nor the transiting planets make an aspect to any of the natal or progressed planets within the allowable orb, the coming month will be one of minor significance. The areas of life most affected will be the houses holding transiting planets and the one in which the Lunation for that month took place.

11. The Full Moon's action often sets off the promise of the New Moon, or it may add to or alter the events indicated by the New Moon. Sometimes it gives a completely different picture.

12. Solar and Lunar Eclipses also tend to act within the coming month, but have more impact, or are of more importance or serious consequence, depending upon the aspects.

13. The Lunar Eclipse acts like a Full Moon and either adds to or alters the events predicted by the Solar Eclipse. The houses holding the opposition of the Sun and Moon will indicate areas of life in which some future decision, issue, change or compromise will have to be reached.

14. The Eclipse should not always be judged with a negative attitude. If the aspects to natal or progressed planets are favorable, the activity will be to the native's benefit. If the Solar or Lunar Eclipse makes difficult aspects to natal or progressed planets, changes will come through drastic or forced actions.

15. One final bit of information: if the New Moon conjuncts or aspects in any way a transiting planet such as Mars for example, watch the transiting movements of Mars during the succeeding four weeks for any aspect that might be made to the native's natal or progressed planets. This can culminate the action promised by the Lunation which was in aspect with transiting Mars.

In the case of Full Moons, the time element holds for the succeeding two weeks; at that time the next New Moon goes into effect.

The same holds for a New or Full Moon aspecting natal or progressed planets. Should the New Moon conjunct natal Uranus in Leo in the natal second house of money for example, watch natal Uranus during the next four weeks for the time that the transiting Moon or Sun forms an aspect to Uranus and thus sets off the promise of the New or Full Moon.

Timing of New and Full Moons

One aspect seldom creates an event of great importance.

If, for example, the New Moon falls in the native's eighth house and he is expecting a refund or dividend check, he will NOT receive it during the four weeks following the New Moon unless one of the aspects listed below takes place at the time of the New Moon.

• The New Moon favorably aspects the natal or transiting ruler of

the eighth house cusp.
- The New Moon in the eighth house favorably aspects natal or transiting Pluto, natural ruler of the eighth house.
- The transiting planet which is the ruler of the native's eight house cusp is favorably aspecting a natal planet.
- The natal ruler of the eighth house cusp is receiving a soft aspect from a transiting planet.
- Natal Pluto, natural ruler of the eighth house, receives soft aspects form a transiting planet.
- Transiting Pluto, natural ruler of the eighth house, makes a soft aspect to one of the native's natal planets.

Without one or more of the above configurations, the New Moon's position in the eighth house merely indicates that a refund or dividend check is forthcoming, but not during the next four weeks.

Look ahead to when the next New Moon favorably highlights the ruler of the eighth house cusp.

However, when both the natal planet ruling the natal or progressed eighth house cusp and the transiting planet which rules the natal or progressed eighth house cusp are favorably aspected simultaneously during one of the forthcoming New Moons, rest assured it is a double confirmation that the refund check should reach the native within the following four weeks. For example, transiting Mars, ruler of the native's natal eight house cusp is trining a natal planet. At the same time, natal Mars, ruler of the native's eighth house cusp, is receiving a sextile or trine aspect from another transiting planet. Both rulers of the natal eighth house cusp are highlighted on the same day.

If, for example, the native is expecting something from a distance, there always will be more than one confirmation. Either the New Moon will take place in the native's ninth house or favorably aspect the ruler of the native's ninth house cusp from a different house position. Or, the transiting planet that rules the native's natal ninth house cusp will favorably aspect a natal planet. Sometimes natal or transiting Jupiter (natural ruler of ninth house matters) or a natal or transiting planet in Sagittarius will be highlighted.

It is the role of the Full Moon to confirm or deny the trends promised by the New Moon. The New Moon can indicate favorable trends for receiving an unexpected refund check, but the Full Moon may throw a few hindering blocks with hard aspects that either will delay or reduce the amount expected.

So bear in mind that all trends indicated by the New Moon will not always take place within the following four weeks. It may take a few months of working with Lunations before being able to project coming events with greater accuracy.

Solar and Lunar Eclipses

Solar and Lunar Eclipses have more far reaching effects than ordinary New and Full Moons. The role of Solar and Lunar Eclipses is to time progressed aspects which are in force during the year ahead.

However, in many instances it will be discovered that Solar and Lunar Eclipses can indicate important events even though there are no apparent aspects between natal and progressed planets.

Timing of Solar and Lunar Eclipses

1. Exactly three months after a Solar and Lunar Eclipse, the New and Full Moon will reach a sign and degree that will square the Eclipse position. For example, a Solar Eclipse on December 24, 1992 was at 2 Capricorn 28 and the Lunar Eclipse of December 9, 1992 was at 18 Gemini 10. For some individuals, Christmas and New Year's was a depressing time as they may have experienced the sorrowful loss of a parent or other older member of the family (Solar Eclipse in Capricorn rules older people). But much depends on the major transits (Jupiter, Saturn, Uranus, Neptune and Pluto) and what they were doing to one's natal or progressed planets. Others suffered a loss or experienced a depressing and important event during March when the New Moon of March 23, 1993 occurred at 2 degrees Aries, exactly squaring the Solar Eclipse position of December 24, 1992 at two degrees Capricorn, and the Full Moon of March 11, 1993 at 17 Virgo 50 squared the Lunar Eclipse of December 9, 1992 at 18 Gemini 10.

2. Others were not affected by the Lunar Eclipse of December 9, 1992 until shortly after the New Moon of April 21, 1993 at 2 degrees Taurus, which would have semi-squared the Lunar Eclipse position at 18 degrees Gemini.

Apparently the major transits were making harder and closer aspects during this period of time to the charts of those affected during the latter part of April. The rule of thumb is to place the Solar Eclipse and all the transits of that day around the natal and progressed charts (be sure to date the Eclipse). Do the same with the Lunar Eclipse around a different set of natal and progressed charts, also including the date. Continue to watch these two charts at the time of each New and Full Moon. Note any important transits during the New or Full Moon period that are highlighting the aspects formed between the previous Eclipse and transits to natal or progressed planets at that time. This is why events promised by the previous Solar and Lunar Eclipses will occur at different times for different people. Each individual has his own set of planetary aspects to be activated by a New or Full Moon and the transits.

Additional Tips on Delineation

1. Always correlate the degree and sign position of the New or Full Moon or an Eclipse with its natal or progressed house position. This is the main starting point of activity for the month (ordinary New Moon) or year (Solar Eclipse) ahead.

2. Note the ruler of the Lunation's sign position by house, sign and aspects thereto.

3. There is greater impact on the event in question whenever the New or Full Moon or an Eclipse aspects the ruler of its sign position within the allowable orb. For example, the Solar Eclipse of November 21, 1992 at 21 degrees Scorpio will conjunct its transiting sign ruler, Pluto, at 24 degrees Scorpio. There will be greater emphasis in the year ahead for matters concerning mutual funds, social security, retirement funds, investments, banking institutions, sex, AIDS, and in extreme cases with very hard aspects, possible loss of someone. Why so important? Because the Eclipse is conjunct the ruler of its sign position. Another example is the New moon of December 13, 1993 at 21 degrees Sagittarius in semi-square aspect with its ruler, Jupiter, at six degrees Scorpio. Those who are involved in a lawsuit (Sagittarius/Jupiter) may have to settle for less than what they expected (New Moon semi-square Jupiter in Scorpio). Some may be upset when college tuition increases greatly.

4. There are only two times not to watch the ruler of the Lunation's sign position: when it takes place in the signs of Leo or Cancer. The Sun and Moon ARE the rulers of the Lunation's sign position and therefore only the aspect the New or Full Moon makes to natal or progressed Sun and Moon can be weighed.

5. There are times when the Lunar Eclipse occurs BEFORE the Solar Eclipse. In this case the conditions of the previous (ordinary) New Moon have to be weighed for clues as to how the Lunar Eclipse would affect the native's natal or progressed chart. For example, the Lunar Eclipse of December 9, 1992 at 18 degrees Gemini took place BEFORE the Solar Eclipse of December 24, 1992 at two degrees Capricorn. That means the New Moon of November 24, 1992 at two degrees Sagittarius has to be given serious consideration with respect to the condition of the next Lunar Eclipse. And the (ordinary) Full Moon of January 8, 1993 at 18 degrees Cancer affords a clue to how the Solar Eclipse of December 24, 1992 would manifest in the natal or progressed chart. Note that the Full Moon of January 8, 1993 at 18 degrees Cancer made an inconjunct to transiting Venus at 18 degrees Aquarius on the day of the Solar Eclipse of December 24 at two degrees Capricorn. Some natives may have been concerned with older, female family members during the coming months.

6. An ordinary New or Full Moon can create a turning point in one's life if the New or Full Moon makes an aspect to a transiting planet within one degree orb while at the same time that transiting planet is in aspect within one degree orb with a natal or progressed planet. For example, the New Moon of June 20, 1993 at 28 degrees Gemini exactly sextiled transiting Mars at 28 degrees Leo. A native with a natal or progressed planet at 28 degrees Aquarius (Mars in opposition while the New Moon trined) or Sagittarius (Mars trine while the New Moon is in opposition) or Aries (Mars trine and the New Moon sextile) or Libra (Mars sextile while the New Moon trined) are just some of the best possible aspects. A natal or progressed planet at 28 degrees Pisces would require adjustments and adaptation to new, changing and upsetting conditions as the New Moon squared and Mars was inconjunct the planet in Pisces.

7. Always use a separate chart for natal and progressed planets. The Lunation will be in different house positions in the natal and progressed charts. One cannot rely solely on natal charts for life's potentials as the progressed chart introduces new people, circumstances and events as individuals grow, mature and reach out to experience them.

8. You can zoom in on one area of life when two planets, one in transit and the other either natal or progressed, are aspected simulta-

neously at the time of a Lunation. For example, transiting Mars makes an aspect to a natal planet at the same time that natal Mars is receiving an aspect from another transiting planet. Depending upon the tone of the two aspects, the native will experience in the weeks ahead the individual, circumstances or events ruled by the house with Aries on its cusp. If for example Aries is on the second house cusp, then money will be of prime importance according to the planets in aspect with both transiting and natal Mars and their sign positions.

9. There is great importance placed upon natal and progressed aspects when all three planets of the same energy are highlighted (see the last chart illustrated in this book). This native had natal Neptune square her Ascendant, a Lunar Eclipse square her progressed Neptune and the Full Moon, prior to a serious illness, was at 11 degrees Aries, exactly squaring transiting Neptune at 11 degrees Capricorn. Although none of these three planets was aspected on the same day so to speak, nevertheless they were of greater importance because one was a progressed aspect, the other aspected by an Eclipse and the last aspected by a Full Moon. All three Neptunes received hard aspects.

10. Always keep a watchful eye on two planets in aspect with one another when they both rule the same house cusp, one a natal house cusp and the other a progressed house cusp. The last two chart illustrations in this book offer excellent examples of this kind of aspect configuration.

11. The more aspects (between transits and natal or progressed planets) in force at the time of an Eclipse or an ordinary Lunation, the greater the impact will be on one's natal or progressed chart. This is especially true if there are two or more major transiting planets involved (Jupiter, Saturn, Uranus, Neptune or Pluto).

Note: Throughout this book the minutes of the planetary positions were omitted in many cases to keep the charts simple and make them easier to read. This was done only for publication purposes.

For additional information about derivative houses (used throughout this book), consult the book From One House to Another *by Sophia Mason.*

The "2-in-1" chart form is available from the American Federation of Astrologers, PO Box 22040, Tempe, AZ 85285-2040.

Second House
New Moon Eclipse

On April 29, 1976 a Solar Eclipse took place in this native's natal second house of money at 9 degrees Taurus. The Eclipse squared natal Mars in the sixth house at 11 degrees Leo, and Mars, ruler of the second house, also opposed transiting Uranus in Scorpio (eighth house matters) in the eighth house of other people's money. With Uranus ruling the Ascendant, the native could have an accident during the ensuing month which would call for added insurance coverage.

The progressed chart confirmed this as the Solar Eclipse took place in the progressed twelfth house opposite progressed Uranus in the sixth house at 4 degrees Scorpio. This brought sixth and twelfth house matters into view. Transiting Venus (ruler of the progressed Ascendant) at 26 degrees Aries was also in the twelfth house and squared transiting Saturn at 26 degrees Cancer in the accident prone third house.

Transiting Venus at 26 degrees Aries is ruler of the natal third house of accidents and the natal eighth house of insurance. It was square transiting Saturn (ruler of the natal twelfth house of hospitals) at 26 degrees Cancer. The charts confirmed one another in respect to twelfth and third house matters. However, transiting Uranus, ruler of the Ascendant, trined natal Sun from the eighth house of death, providing a protective influence and saving the native from serious harm.

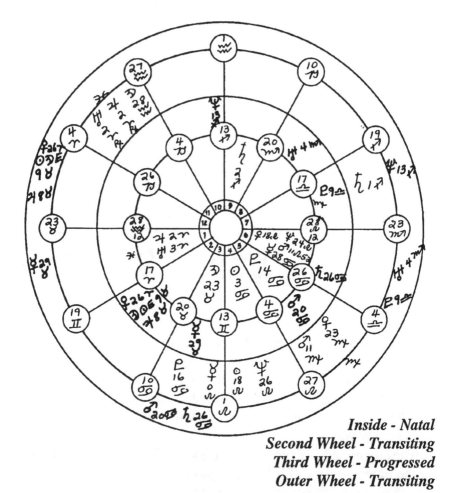

Inside - Natal
Second Wheel - Transiting
Third Wheel - Progressed
Outer Wheel - Transiting

The Solar Eclipse in the progressed twelfth house trined progressed Mars in the fifth house of children. It was a young man of 16-years-old who caused the accident; he, too, escaped with no serious injuries. The Solar Eclipse was too far out of orb to square the progressed Sun at 18 degrees Leo as the maximum allowance is 5 degrees orb to both natal and progressed planets.

Prior to the accident, the native called her auto insurance company and added coverage for uninsured motorists and collision, the only two coverages she did not carry. Nothing happened during the first two weeks after the Solar Eclipse, but the accident did occur the day after the Lunar Eclipse at 22 degrees Scorpio.

The young man was driving a truck (transiting Saturn in the

progressed third indicates heavy equipment such as trucks) and ran a red light as the native was driving through on the green. The native hit the truck full force, demolishing the entire front end of her new car. The Solar Eclipse at 9 degrees Taurus squared natal Mars in Leo, indicating an accident with a young person (Leo) and, as the Solar Eclipse in the progressed chart trined progressed Mars in the fifth of children, the young man was not harmed. Much to everyone's surprise, the native also escaped without any serious injuries (Uranus trined her Natal Sun).

Although it was a company owned truck, the young man was not driving it for company purposes; therefore the insurance company would not cover the accident. This was the opposition between the natal second and eighth houses which, to say it simply, means my money or yours. Later, the native's insurance company did some research and discovered that the parents of the young man had him insured under their policy, which further protected the native. The Solar Eclipse conjunct transiting Jupiter in the native's natal second house of money delayed the benefits because the conjunction took place in the progressed twelfth, indicating that matters to do with insurance (transiting Jupiter rules the eighth house of insurance in the progressed chart) would undergo some delay due to a confusing element over insurance coverage.

The Full Moon or Lunar Eclipse on May 13, 1976 took place at 22 degrees Scorpio in the natal ninth house, and the Sun at 22 degrees Taurus was in the natal third conjunct the natal Moon. Both Sun and Moon squared natal Neptune at 24 degrees Leo in the sixth house. Not only was the native taken to the hospital for examination of possible internal injuries or concussion, but she met her sister there. Her sister had been taken in an hour earlier for a serious health problem about which physicians were having trouble detecting the cause. The Lunar Eclipse opposed natal Moon in the third house (sister) and squared natal Neptune (hidden) in the sixth house (illness).

Looking back at the Solar Eclipse, note that transiting Venus at 26 degrees Aries was in the natal second house (the twelfth house from the third house of sisters) and squared transiting Saturn, which rules the native's twelfth house of hospitals. Venus also rules the third house of brothers and sisters in the natal chart and transiting Saturn was heading for a conjunction with natal Mercury (ruler of brothers and sisters) at 28 degrees Cancer. In the progressed chart, transiting Venus squared transiting Saturn at 26 degrees Cancer in the progressed third, indicating that sometime during Saturn's two and one-half year stay in the progressed third, there would be serious concern for brothers, sisters, or those in the immediate family. It took aspects occurring at the Solar Eclipse to activate this position of Saturn.

The day after the Lunar Eclipse on May 14, transiting Saturn and transiting Mars both reached an exact conjunction wtih natal Mercury. Transiting Mercury in the third house was retrograde at 2 degrees Gemini (Mercury and Gemini govern brothers, sisters and close relations) opposing natal Saturn at 2 degrees Sagittarius, indicating serious concern over matters to do with close relations.

In the progressed chart, the May 13 Lunar Eclipse at 22 degrees Scorpio occurred in the sixth house of health and sextiled progressed Venus at 23 degrees Virgo in the progressed fifth house, indicating the second oldest sister.

The Lunar Eclipse opposing the natal Moon and squaring natal Neptune indicated that a close relative might enter the hospital. All the action from the third house - Venus (ruler of the natal third house) at 26 degrees squaring transiting Saturn at 26 degrees Cancer and transiting Saturn in the progressed third - pointed to a sister. An unusual configuration which was entirely overlooked in the chart at the time of the Lunar Eclipse was transiting Mercury at 2 degrees Gemini opposing natal Saturn at 2 degrees Sagittarius in the ninth house; a double configuration of concern about in-laws.

In the progressed chart, transiting Venus in the twelfth house squaring transiting Saturn in third house brought about serious news of a brother or sister-in-law because Saturn rules the progressed ninth house. This also was indicated by the Lunar Eclipse that occurred in the natal second house, which is the brother-in-law's health (the ninth house from the sixth house).

The eclipse squared natal Mars (surgery) in Leo (heart), and a brother-in-law had open heart surgery on the day the transiting Moon left the opposition of the eclipse and entered into the second house just before the next New Moon.

Fourth House Lunation

On January 31, 1976, the Lunation took place at 10 degrees Aquarius in the native's fourth house which governs the home, family, breast and stomach. The chart discloses a touching incident in the life of a fine young woman, adored by her husband and children, who suddenly discovered she had cancer in one breast. Her Libra Ascendant was appalled at the idea of being disfigured even if it meant saving her life.

The natal Moon at 9 degrees Pisces opposed natal Neptune at 7 degrees Virgo and both were in a T-square with natal Mercury (she can harbor secretive fears because of natal Moon in Pisces square mental Mercury and opposition Neptune, which tends to distort her rational thinking), square Venus, her ruling planet (sees beauty in many things), and square natal Mars, ruler of her sixth house of health (she had secret fears of surgery and disfigurement).

Checking the pros and cons of the aspects from the Lunation and transiting planets to both natal and progressed charts, removal of the breast is definite, however it would not be radical and the promise is there for a speedy recovery. Remember, for a serious incident to take place in one's life, progressed planets, the tenth house cusp or the progressed Ascendant must be aspecting natal planets.

Look at her progressed planets. The progressed Moon was at 16 degrees Libra forming a square with progressed Mars at 17 degrees Capricorn in opposition with natal Uranus at 16 degrees Aries in the

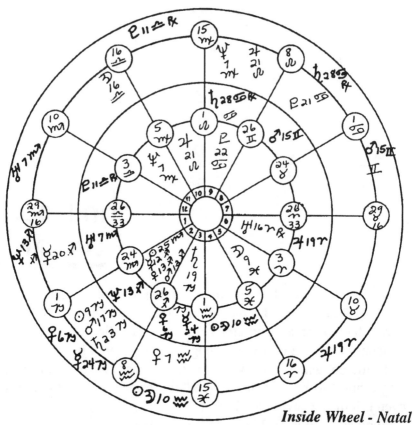

Inside Wheel - Natal
Second Wheel - Transiting
Third Wheel - Progressed
Outer Wheel - Transiting

sixth house of health; Mars is the ruler of the sixth house. Progressed Mars at 17 degrees Capricorn had formed a square to natal Uranus for several years, but it took the progressed Moon and the New Moon to set off the progressed aspect.

At first it looked as though the native would undergo an unexpected and upsetting job change (Mars in Capricorn ruling work and Uranus in the sixth house of work), but there were too many Neptunian influences. Both the sixth and twelfth houses were greatly activated.

What is meant by too many Neptunian influences?

• Transiting Uranus at 7 degrees Scorpio in the progressed twelfth house (hospitals) sextile progressed Neptune (natural ruler of hospitals).

- Transiting Pluto in the tenth house, ruler of the progressed twelfth house (hospitals) was brought into action by a trine from the New Moon.

- Pluto (ruler of the progressed twelfth house) was transiting through the native's natal twelfth house of hospitals. These are strong indicators of hospital visits which will result in some change concerning the body or an elimination of some sort; Pluto rules change and elimination).

- Transiting Neptune (ruler of hospitals) was conjunct Mars, ruler of the natal sixth house, and natal Venus, ruler of the Ascendant and the twelfth house; natal Mercury also was included in the conjunction. Mercury rules the ninth house of legal affairs and the native had to sign a legal document consenting to the surgery.

The Lunation at 10 degrees Aquarius took place in her progressed third house which meant that decisions would have to be made. Progressed Venus (ruler of her progressed sixth house of health) at 7 degrees Aquarius, was squared by transiting Uranus at 7 degrees Scorpio in her twelfth house of hospitals. An unexpected decision (Venus in progressed third in Aquarius) would have to be made concerning health (Venus rules the sixth), which would result in a quick trip to the hospital as indicated by transiting Uranus in the twelfth house at 7 degrees Scorpio square Venus (Uranus rules sudden unexpected trips and Scorpio rules surgery).

In the natal chart, the New Moon at 10 degrees Aquarius trined transiting Pluto in the natal twelfth house and transiting Mars at 15 degrees Gemini in the eighth house (surgery), indicating that although the breast might have to be removed (Pluto rules removals) the surgery would have no serious effect on the muscles (Mars) controlling the usage of her hands (Gemini). As it turned out, no therapy was needed even though this is often the case with a breast removal.

Transiting Neptune on the day of the Lunation was conjunct natal Mercury, the planet of the mind, which gave her a mental obsession that she would not survive. Mental depression was compounded by transiting Mercury at 24 degrees Capricorn conjunct progressed Saturn at 23 degrees Capricorn, indicating a serious and depressive state of mind.

The favorable aspects pointing to a non-radical surgery and an easy recovery were the Lunation in the fourth house (governs the breast); sextile natal Mars at 13 degrees Sagittarius, ruler of the sixth house of health; sextile Venus at 13 degrees Sagittarius, ruler of the Ascendant and natal eighth house of surgery; and sextile Mercury at 13 degrees Sagittarius. She would eventually make a rational decision and sign the required legal documents (Mercury rules the ninth). A further indication was that the Lunation trined both transiting Mars at 15 degrees Gemini, ruler of the sixth house, and transiting Pluto in the native's twelfth house.

The native had surgery on February 11, 1976, prior to which she was strongly opposed signing the consent forms. Transiting Venus at 19 degrees Capricorn (ruler of the natal chart and the natal eighth house of surgery) was exactly conjunct her natal Saturn in the natal third house of mental attitude. At the same time, transiting Mercury at 26 degrees Capricorn was in the third house opposing transiting Saturn at 27 degrees Cancer in the ninth house. These are two aspects of heavy mental depression and the native was convinced she was going to die (Venus ruler of the natal eighth). She signed the necessary papers when the transiting Moon entered 26 degrees Gemini to conjunct her ninth house cusp and trine her natal Ascendant. On that day transiting Mars was at 17 degrees Gemini in the natal eighth house of surgery and trining her progressed Moon, and she became convinced that signing the legal documents concerning sixth house matters (Mars and surgery) would be a wise decision.

The native's breast was completely removed, but the lymph nodes and muscles of the arm were not. Her hands and arms were not affected as was indicated by the Lunation's trine to transiting Mars in Gemini. Her recovery and mental attitude was astounding and far better than anticipated because of the strong encouragement received from her husband, children, physician and astrologer (the author).

She was well versed in the field of astrology and looked to her astrologer for guidance and assurance; honesty was the only approach. However, complete honesty must be tempered with optimism and encouragement. She wanted so much to hear that the lump in her breast would not be serious and a breast removal would not be necessary, but had this author lied to her, she would not have been trusted again.

The only course of action for this author was to go to the hospital, show her the chart along with all the heavy aspects and the favorable ones, and draw her a picture of excellent recovery with a full life ahead. It was not easy for a Libra Ascendant to accept such a decision and this author's heart went out to her when she came out of surgery and exclaimed to her husband with tears in her eyes, "Oh! I have a special bandage. That means it had to be removed."

No matter what the chart may disclose, it is important to always maintain an optimistic attitude and look for any ray of sunshine that may help others overcome their fears.

Uranus (ruler of the fourth house governing the breast) at 16 degrees Aries in the natal sixth house of health trined natal Mars (ruler of the sixth house) at 13 degrees Sagittarius, indicating that radiation treatments would be advisable along with surgery. Mars rules surgery and Uranus rules radiation treatments, especially when positioned in the natal sixth house. In this case Uranus promises excellent results from radiation treatments due to the fact that it trines the ruler of the sixth house.

Sixth and Tenth House Lunation

The two charts are of district managers for a large corporation. Chart A received a promotion with a substantial increase in salary; Chart B was terribly disappointed.

The Lunation occurred February 29, 1976 at 10 degrees Pisces in Chart A's natal sixth house of work. Even a novice astrologer should be able to read the potential from the Lunation trining the natal Sun at 10 degrees Cancer, Venus at 10 degrees Cancer and natal Pluto at 10 degrees Cancer - all in the tenth house of career. Natal Venus rules both the natal Ascendant and the eighth house of money belonging to others (a bonus). The Sun rules his eleventh house, which indicates money earned through one's profession (the second house from the tenth house), and Pluto rules his second house of personal finances. All promised monetary increases. The Lunation trined transiting Uranus in his natal second house, indicating that the increase in income would come unexpectedly.

And, with the Lunation sextiling his natal Moon (ruler of his tenth house of career) at 12 degrees Capricorn, all aspects clearly pointed to a month of exciting changes in his career and financial status, all of which did occur. However, the promotion was kept a secret (Lunation in Pisces) from his co-worker and partner, (Lunation in the natal sixth house of co-workers) until later.

In the progressed chart the Lunation at 10 degrees Pisces took place in the fourth house (a new beginning or completion of an old matter)

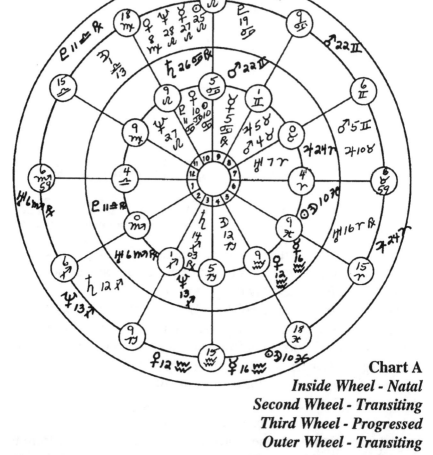

Chart A
Inside Wheel - Natal
Second Wheel - Transiting
Third Wheel - Progressed
Outer Wheel - Transiting

and trined the conjunction of his progressed Ascendant and transiting Uranus at 6 degrees Scorpio. The Lunation hinted that there were hidden or secretive matters behind it (Pisces) and it opposed progressed Venus (ruler of the seventh house of partnerships) at 8 degrees Virgo (co-worker) in the progressed tenth house and sqaure progressed Mars (ruler of the sixth house of co-workers) at 5 degrees Gemini in the seventh house of partners.

Something beneficial (Lunation trined planets in the natal chart) to do with career matters and the native (Lunation trined Ascendant and transiting Uranus) but totally unexpected and at the expense of a co-worker or partner which would be kept a secret (Lunation in Pisces) from the co-worker (Lunation in natal sixth house) was

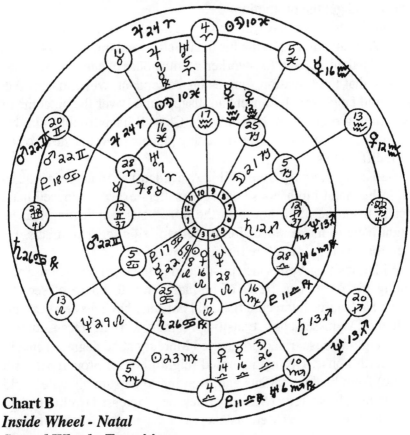

Chart B
Inside Wheel - Natal
Second Wheel - Transiting
Third Wheel - Progressed
Outer Wheel - Transiting

indicated. This native was given control (Pluto in natal tenth house) of a new department in a new branch with a substantial increase in salary (Pluto rules the second house of money).

The Lunation in the district manager's Chart B took place in his tenth house of career, and squared natal Saturn in the sixth house of co-workers and transiting Neptune in his seventh of partnerships. The native of chart A was his co-worker as well as his business partner. Neptune rules the district manager's eleventh house of friends and he considered this man to be a close friend, fully unaware that his co-worker and friend was working behind his back with a boss (Lunation in Pisces in the tenth house governing bosses) to determine who would get the promotion.

Both his boss and co-worker kept it a secret as was disclosed in Chart A's Lunation squaring his natal Saturn and transiting Neptune in his Natal third house (co-worker's tenth house of careers). In Chart B, note that the Lunation squares his Ascendant, which means that he would be personally upset and disappointed over the outcome of the pending promotion. Not only did Chart B have trouble with his job, but the placements of the transiting planets show that he also had legal difficulties.

Transiting Mercury (ruler of his Ascendant) at 16 degrees Aquarius in his natal ninth house of legal matters exactly opposed natal Venus from the ninth house to the third house, indicating that he might have to make a decision or perhaps sign legal contracts. He filed for divorce just before the next New Moon.

With transiting Venus also positioned in the natal ninth house and trining his Ascendant (ruler of his natal twelfth house of secrets, which has Taurus intercepted), he did not deny having a secret affair.

In the progressed chart, transiting Mercury at 16 degrees Aquarius in the eighth house trined progressed Mercury at 16 degrees Libra in the fourth house. He had inherited (eighth house) property (fourth house) from his late parents and, wanting to be sure his wife could not claim it, he secretly (Mercury rules the progressed twelfth house) consulted an attorney (Mercury also rules the progressed third house) concerning the property (Mercury in progressed fourth house in Libra, which governs lawyers) to make sure the deed (Mercury in the fourth house) was in his name alone. The trine from the transiting eighth house Mercury to the progressed fourth house Mercury assured him that it was.

There was one more important and serious event concerning the district manager (Chart B). By applying the techniques from this author's book *From One House to Another* to the Lunation which took place in Chart B's tenth house, it is easy to see how a boss or superior would suffer sorrow or be seriously concerned about his children and his sister. In the natal ninth house, transiting Mercury at 16 degrees Aquarius (something unexpected) indicates sorrow (the ninth house is the twelfth house from the boss' tenth house) concerning children; Mercury opposes Venus in Leo and Mercury rules the fifth house, which is the boss' eighth house of death. Also, because

24

Venus rules the natal twelfth, which is the boss' third house of brothers and sisters, a sister (Venus) could be involved.

Transiting Neptune was conjunct progressed Saturn, which rules the ninth (the twelfth house of sorrows of the boss), and both planets opposed the Ascendant, which is the boss's fourth house of home.

In the progressed chart, the Lunation at 10 degrees Pisces was in the ninth house (the twelfth house from the boss' tenth house) and squared both progressed Saturn in the fifth house (the boss' eighth house) and transiting Neptune, which rules the progressed ninth house, sorrow and hospital matters of the tenth house boss.

In the progressed chart, note that transiting Mars is exactly conjunct progressed Mars at 22 degrees Gemini in the twelfth house (the third house from the boss' tenth house). In the natal chart, transiting Mars was in the natal first house (the fourth house from the boss' tenth house).

What happened? There was a fire in the boss' home and his sister, who was living with him at the time (transiting Mars in Gemini in the twelfth house, which is the third house from the boss' tenth house and in the natal first house, and the fourth house from the boss' tenth house and in Gemini, indicating a close relation) taking care of his two children plus one of her own, died in the fire along with his two children. The only survivor was his sister's child.

Looking at the progressed third house, which is the boss' sixth house, the progressed Sun was at 23 degrees Virgo and being squared by both progressed Mars and transiting Mars conjunct at 22 degrees Gemini with Mars ruling the progressed tenth house of bosses; the Sun rules the progressed second house which is the boss' fifth house of children.

There were several aspects to show the survival of his sister's child. Transiting Mercury at 16 degrees Aquarius (natural ruler of brothers and sisters) in the progressed eighth house trined progressed Mercury in the fourth house, which is the fifth house from the twelfth house (the twelfth house is the third house from the tenth house boss). Transiting Venus in the progressed seventh house at 12 degrees Aquarius trined transiting Pluto at 11 degrees Libra in the progressed fourth house. The seventh house is the eighth house from the twelfth house (the third house from the tenth house) and Venus trined Pluto in the fourth house (the fifth house from the twelfth house), thus saving his sister's child.

Look at Chart A and apply the principals from the book *From One House to Another* to see the amazing similarity of aspects indicating the same loss in that chart.

In the progressed chart of Chart A, transiting Uranus at 6 degrees Scorpio is conjunct the progressed Ascendant; this is the fourth house from the tenth house boss, indicating unexpected events occurring in the home. In the natal chart transiting Uranus is in the second house, the fifth house from the boss' tenth house concerning his children.

Did Chart A like his promotion?

The next month's Lunation, which took place on March 30, 1976 at 10 degrees Aries, created a cardinal cross in his chart by conjuncting natal Uranus at 7 degrees Aries, squaring natal Moon at 12 degrees Capricorn (ruler of his tenth house), and opposing transiting Pluto in the natal first house; all three planets were in adverse aspect with natal Sun, Venus and Pluto in the tenth house. Much to his dismay, he discovered unexpectedly (Uranus) that his new boss (Sun, Venus and Pluto in the tenth house) was a domineering woman.

As is indicated, the natal chart may relate one set of circumstances while the progressed chart still another; in many other cases they often confirm each other in related events.

Seventh House Solar Eclipse

This is the chart of an osteopath who was found guilty and sentenced to prison for murdering his wife.

The Solar Eclipse took place on June 30, 1954 at 8 degrees Cancer in his natal seventh house of marriage and partnerships. It was conjunct natal Pluto, ruler of his natal eleventh house, which is his wife's fifth house of children; she was pregnant at the time of her death. The New Moon Eclipse was also conjunct transiting Jupiter, ruler of his natal Ascendent, indicating that he might be personally involved in some way with her death.

There were many outstanding confirmations that death would be imminent during the ensuing month. First, the Lunation was conjunct natal Pluto, natural ruler of death. Second, the Lunation also opposed his natal Sun at 6 degrees Capricorn, ruler of his eighth house of death. Transiting Venus at 15 degrees Leo was positioned in the natal eighth house and square natal Mars at 16 degrees Scorpio, a sign that normally is affiliated with death. Other configurations were transiting Uranus, ruler of the second house, his wife's eighth house, positioned in his eighth house and square transiting Neptune in the natal tenth house of public scandal (Neptune rules scandals).

Was he guilty? The reader will have to be the judge of that, however Jupiter (ruling planet) was involved in the conjunction of the Solar Eclipse and his natal Pluto. Transiting Jupiter also was quincunx his progressed Sun at 7 degrees Aquarius in his first house,

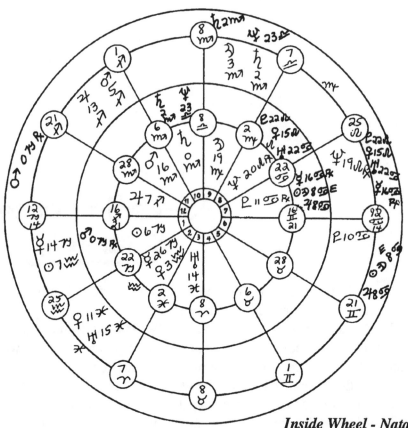

Inside Wheel - Natal
Second Wheel - Transiting
Third Wheel - Progressed
Outer Wheel - Transiting

ruler of his wife's eighth house of death.

In the progressed chart the Solar Eclipse at 8 degrees Cancer took place in his sixth house of co-workers and trined progressed Venus in Pisces; it became apparent he was having a clandestine affair with a co-worker at the hospital where he practiced and court testimony confirmed this. Progressed aspects also substantiated this with progressed Venus at 11 degrees Pisces trining natal Pluto (sexual) in Cancer (emotional involvement). This is not to imply that everyone with progressed Venus entering Pisces will have a secret affair, but when Venus also makes any aspect to a planet that rules the twelfth house in the natal or progressed chart, this does add fuel to the fire and rather confirms the element of hidden intrigue.

The progressed aspect of Venus in Pisces trine his natal Pluto in the seventh house would also account for the fact that his wife was pregnant. There were accusations that this child was not his, but with Venus in Pisces (something hidden) and trining natal Pluto, ruler of the secretive twelfth, no one will ever know for sure.

Although he was later exonerated, the mystery behind the death would forever remain a secret. Transiting Uranus (ruler of the natal second house and his wife's eighth house) in the natal eighth house indicated something unexpected, perhaps in the way of death, would occur. Uranus squared Neptune (secrecy involved in the death) in Libra (his wife) and the events surrounding the death would cost him loss of reputation through a scandal (transiting Neptune in the natal tenth house).

The only incident of death in the progressed chart was transiting Saturn conjunct progressed Saturn and progressed Moon at 2 degrees and 3 degrees Scorpio in the progressed ninth house of legal affairs and courts. With both transiting and progressed Saturn activated by the progressed Moon, and Saturn the ruler of his progressed Ascendant, something was bound to occur during this period of conjunctions. He could become involved in some kind of legal problem either to do with money belonging to others (Scorpio element) or death. The entire chart must be taken into consideration to determine which might be the case.

His progressed chart speaks mainly of his secret affair, for another indication of this was transiting Mercury (ruler of the progressed sixth house) at 16 degrees Cancer trine progressed Uranus at 15 degrees Pisces; the sixth house also indicates a co-worker, perhaps more than one.

There is yet another progressed aspect that gives food for thought. Progressed Jupiter in the eleventh house at 13 degrees Sagittarius squared natal Uranus in the third house of brothers and close relations at 14 degrees Pisces. Was it possible that his wife had been carrying his brother's child? The eleventh house is the fifth house from the seventh house of marriage partner, his wife's fifth house of children. Both Jupiter and Sagittarius rule in-laws and Mars in Sagittarius indicates a male in-law. Progressed Jupiter squared natal Uranus (unexpected), indicating an event which had to remain secret (Uranus in Pisces) because he was his brother-in-law (Uranus in the third house is the ninth house of in-laws from the seventh of marriage partners). Whatever the case may be, his brothers will stand behind him and help keep all incidents secret because Neptune rules the natal third of brothers and close relations and transiting Neptune at 23 degrees Libra in the tenth house squared transiting Uranus at 22 degrees Cancer in the eighth house, ruler of the natal second which is the brother's twelfth house of secrets. His brothers will never reveal matters to do with her death or her pregnancy.

Not only does this Lunation at 8 degrees Cancer indicate death of his wife but, looking a little deeper into the transiting planets and their condition, another is spotted.

Transiting Venus in the natal eighth house in Leo squared natal Mars at 16 degrees Scorpio within the one degree allowable orb. Venus in Leo indicates a young child and, as the ruler of his natal fifth house, this would endorse the fact. It would be death through surgery for Venus squares Mars (ruler of surgery) in Scorpio (death was the result). He operated on a young boy who was hit by a truck, but the surgery was unsuccessful and the child died on the operating table on July 3 when transiting Moon at 16 degrees Leo in the eighth house squared natal Mars at 16 degrees Scorpio and was conjunct transiting Venus in the eighth house at 18 degrees Leo. The bludgeon death of his wife took place on the next day, July 4, while the transiting Moon was still positioned in his natal eighth house.

The incident took place early in the morning while the transiting Moon was at 26 degrees Leo and quincunx natal Mercury at 26 degrees Capricorn, ruler of the natal seventh house and positioned in the natal second house, his wife's eighth house of death.

Also on July 4, transiting Sun, ruler of the natal eighth house, was in the seventh house of marriage partner conjunct natal Pluto at 11 degrees Cancer. Transiting Mercury retrograded to 14 degrees Cancer in the progressed seventh house and opposed progressed Mercury at 14 degrees Capricorn in the first house. Mercury, ruler of the natal seventh house and progressed fifth house were his wife and a not yet born child.

He was convicted and found guilty on December 21, 1954. The New Moon prior to December 21 took place on November 25 at 2 degrees Sagittarius in the natal twelfth house of prison and confinement. Transiting Mercury and Venus on that day were at 16 degrees

Scorpio conjunct natal Mars at 16 degrees Scorpio. All three planets ruled the fourth house of final outcome, the natal seventh house of litigation, the ninth house of legal matters and the tenth house of public recognition.

In the progressed chart the progressed Moon was conjunct the progressed tenth house cusp at 8 degrees Scorpio and squared the progressed Sun at 7 degrees Aquarius in the progressed first house, ruler of the progressed eighth house.

The Full Moon added the final blow, taking place in his first and seventh houses at 17 degrees Gemini and Sagittarius, and squaring the natal Moon at 19 degrees Virgo in the ninth house of judges.

Eighth House
Full Moon Eclipse

This chart is an excellent example of certain conditions in the native's character that manifested without anyone being aware of the despondent state that drove him to commit suicide.

Often a slow moving planet such as Neptune will make adverse aspects to the Ascendant or natal and progressed planets for prolonged periods, sometimes lasting up to two years. Nothing significant seems to result from the aspect until a heavy New Moon, Full Moon, progressed Moon or Eclipse sets off the aspect, as was the case in this native's chart.

Many a budding astrologer may experience, for example, transiting Saturn in Leo square natal Sun at 3 degrees Scorpio and perhaps the father may suffer a heart attack. Then transiting Saturn may go as high as 4 degrees or 5 degrees Leo before retrograding to perhaps 1 degree or 2 degrees Leo. The novice astrologer may view the transit of Saturn back to 3 degrees Leo with much apprehension, only to have nothing significant occur. Perhaps, they reason, something will happen when Saturn goes forward to 3 degrees Leo for the last time. Then they become even more puzzled when Saturn not only reaches 3 degrees Leo, but passes it without any reccurrence of the parent's health problem. Often, the situation may be reversed with nothing significant occurring with the first heavy transit aspect and even during the retrograde period, only to experience difficulty at the last transit. What is the answer to this puzzling dilemma? Apparently the

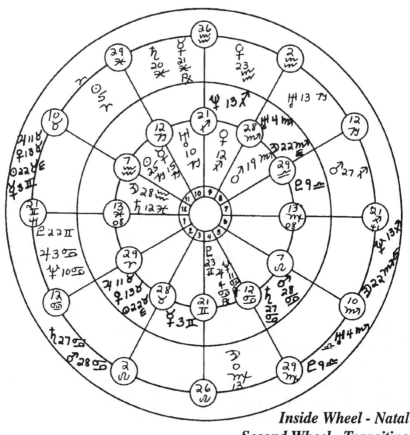

Inside Wheel - Natal
Second Wheel - Transiting
Third Wheel - Progressed
Outer Wheel - Transiting

Lunation, Full Moon, progressed Moon or an Eclipse period was not making any adverse aspects of great significance to either the natal or progressed planets while the heavy transiting planet in question was in the one degree orb of allowance, as was the case in this suicidal death. Transiting Neptune had been hovering over his natal Venus and squaring both natal Saturn and his ascending sign for more than a year or two. It took a Full Moon Eclipse in the natal eighth house to instigate the action towards suicide. Before attempting to work with the Lunation, it is important to first try to understand the mental attitude of the native in question.

There were several progressed planets in action. Progressed retrograde Mercury had reached a conjunction with progressed Saturn at

20 degrees Pisces in the progressed tenth house of career. Both progressed Mercury and Saturn in Pisces squared the progressed Ascendant at 21 degrees Gemini conjunct progressed Pluto at 22 degrees Gemini. This often indicates obsessions with death (Pluto on Ascendant or dread of changes being forced on the native). Progressed Mercury conjunct progressed Saturn in Pisces often creates mental (Mercury) depression (Saturn) coupled with psychological fears or suicidal tendencies (Mercury and Saturn positioned in Pisces).

This is the chart of a recently retired 65-year-old man who was heart sick and mentally depressed over his forced retirement (progressed Mercury and Saturn in the progressed tenth house squared the progressed Ascendant, and Mercury is the ruler of the progressed Ascendant). Thoughts can be harbored in the back of one's mind and nourished until the right Lunation or Full Moon brings the thought or action to reality. Why were we so certain that the Full Moon Eclipse on May 13, 1976 at 22 degrees Scorpio would personally affect the native's health and perhaps endanger his life? Because all three Neptunes - natal, progressed and transiting (Neptune is ruler of his natal Ascendant) - were heavily afflicted, as well as Venus, ruler of his natal eighth house of death and changes.

Look at the Full Moon at 22 degrees Scorpio and notice that it is positioned in the natal eighth house and in a sign that governs death and changes. In the progressed chart, the eclipse took place in the progressed sixth house of health. He was harboring secret thoughts that he was seriously ill and that his family was keeping it from him, even though he was given a clean bill of health through a recent examination. The Eclipse squared progressed Venus, ruler of the progressed twelfth house of secrets and fears.

Transiting Neptune was conjunct natal Venus, ruler of the natal eighth house, which is not necessarily evil except for the fact that Neptune also squared the natal Ascendent and Saturn at 12 degrees Pisces positioned in the twelfth house of secret fears and suicide. There was a second configuration of a secret death wish. Transiting Pluto at 9 degrees Libra formed a T-square with natal Uranus (ruler of the natal twelfth house) at 10 degrees Capricorn and progressed Neptune at 10 degrees Cancer. A third configuration, the quincunx aspect of fate, had transiting Venus (ruler of the eighth hosue) at 13 degrees Taurus quincunx natal Venus and conjunct transiting Neptune at 12 and 13 degrees Sagittarius. Both transiting and natal Venus ruled the natal eighth house and Neptune was ruler of the natal Ascendant.

When transiting Neptune squares one's Ascendant, it causes deception from others, confused thinking, self pity and sometimes a propensity towards an imaginary illness. However, when one's Ascendant happens to be Pisces, as is the case with this gentleman, then conditions become magnified out of proportion because Neptune is also the ruling planet.

Further stress was indicated in his chart by transiting Pluto at 9 degrees Libra squaring natal Uranus at 10 degrees Capricorn in the natal tenth house. This change (Pluto) in his job position (tenth house) was indeed going to be an upsetting one (Uranus).

He committed suicide the next day when the transiting Moon entered Sagittarius and was conjunct both natal Venus and transiting Neptune and also square his natal Ascendant and natal Saturn at 12 degrees Pisces.

As was explained in the introduction, the transiting Moon is the trigger which often sets into motion the action promised by the New or Full Moon.

Every month the transiting Moon was conjunct this individual's natal Venus and square his natal Saturn and Pisces Ascendant. Surely this gentlemen did not consider such drastic ideas of suicide every month. But, when the Lunation or Full Moon and the other transiting planets on the day of the Lunation give the indication, only then will action take place and great importance be placed on the transiting Moon.

Ninth House
Lunar Eclipse

This chart should clarify any negative ideas that all Solar and Lunar Eclipses are ominous in character. It is true, however, that they will react more strongly in the natal or progressed chart than the regular monthly New and Full Moons.

This Lunar Eclipse took place on May 25, 1975 at 3 degrees Sagittarius in the natal ninth house and progressed seventh house. It made no adverse aspects to any natal or progressed planets in the chart, except for the conjunction with natal and progressed Saturn. In fact, the Full Moon Eclipse formed a grand trine to natal and progressed Jupiter at 2 Aries, was conjunct natal and progressed Uranus at 3 degrees Aries and trine progressed Mercury at zero degrees Leo.

It was clear that both this native (Lunar Eclipse trine natal Jupiter and Uranus in the first house) and her husband (Lunar Eclipse in the progressed seventh house) would come before the public as Jupiter rules the natal tenth house and Uranus the first house.

The eclipse promised something more than average circumstances. The native's husband won $15,000 in the state lottery, but was disappointed he did not win one of the larger prizes which were $30,000, $60,000 and $100,000 (Lunar Eclipse conjunct both natal and progressed Saturn: restriction). They appeared before the public (Jupiter rules the tenth house) and on TV (ruled by Uranus).

A look at the transiting planets offers a clue as to why this couple

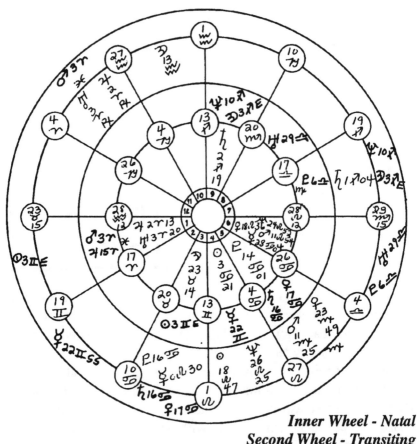

Inner Wheel - Natal
Second Wheel - Transiting
Third Wheel - Progressed
Outer Wheel - Transiting

did not win a larger sum.

The first position to note is transiting Mars at 3 degrees Aries in the natal first house, also involved in the grand trine by conjunction with both natal Jupiter and Uranus (the unexpected good fortune points to money; Mars rules the second house). Transiting Uranus, ruler of the native's Ascendant was in the eighth house of money belonging to others, joint finances, her husband's money and the masses of people that spend their dollars to make the lottery possible. Uranus trined the Ascendant, indicating unexpected good fortune through resources of others. If one looks closely, there always will be more than one confirming aspect pointing to a definite picture.

The picture certainly looked rosy for this couple except for a few hidden thorns in the rose patch. Transiting Mercury (ruler of the progressed second house of money) in the progressed second house at 22 degrees Gemini squared progressed Venus (ruler of the progressed Ascendant) at 23 degrees Virgo in the fifth house of gambling, indicating a disappointment concerning money. Transiting Mars, ruler of the native's natal second house, which also is ruler of the eighth house from her husband's seventh house, was square her natal Sun (ruler of the native's seventh house) at 3 degrees Cancer.

If this were not enough to cut down the size of the winnings, there is even further testimony. Transiting Jupiter in the natal first house at 15 degrees Aries was squared by transiting Saturn at 16 degrees Cancer, which was conjunct transiting Venus at 17 degrees Cancer in the fifth house of gambling. With Venus ruling the natal eighth house and the husband's second house, and the conjunction of transiting Saturn, there was a restriction or limit on the amount of money he would win.

They discovered the win on June 5, 1975 when the transiting Moon entered Aries and the natal second house, fulfilling the promise of the previous Lunar Eclipse trine transiting Mars, ruler of the natal second house of money. Transiting Mars also trined natal Mars.

Eleventh
House Lunation

The January Lunation in 1975 took place at 21 degrees Capricorn in the native's eleventh house of friends, clubs and organizations. This chart was chosen to show how favorable aspects help offset unfavorable ones.

The Lunation created a cardinal cross within the progressed chart by conjuncting progressed Mars at 17 degrees Capricorn in the ninth house of travel, squaring progressed Moon and Jupiter in Libra, opposing progressed Pluto in Cancer in the third house, and squaring progressed Uranus in Aries in the twelfth house; all are accident prone houses.

In the natal chart the Lunation at 21 degrees Capricorn took place in the eleventh house of friends and organizations, opposing natal Uranus in the first house at 24 degrees Aries.

It was clear that something unexpected (Uranus), possibly an accident (Mars) while traveling (Jupiter), would bring about a change of plans or a delay (Pluto).

The first step is to determine the seriousness of the event by checking whether any of the above mentioned planets received favorable aspects. Transiting Mars at 22 degrees Sagittarius in the progressed eighth house trined progressed Uranus in the progressed twelfth house and also sextiled the progressed Moon.

Looks as though things are going to work out.

The Lunation also trined the progressed Ascendant, another im-

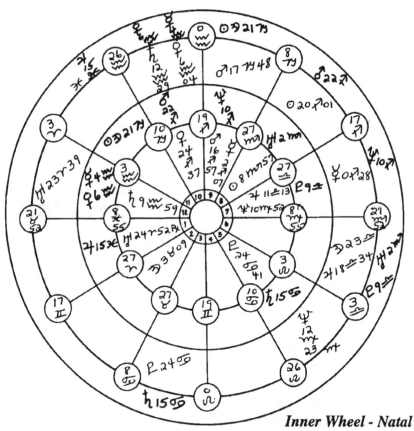

Inner Wheel - Natal
Second Wheel - Transiting
Third Wheel - Progressed
Outer Wheel - Transiting

portant saving grace that would help protect the individual. Transiting Pluto was in exact trine to natal Saturn in Aquarius, ruler of the eleventh house of friends, so her friends would not to be injured either. And, to further protect both the individual and her friends, transiting Jupiter, co-ruler of the natal Ascendant was in the natal first house in exact trine aspect to transiting Saturn, ruler of the eleventh house of friends; the friends were older women. Something was going to happen while traveling with her friends.

Why traveling and with friends? Transiting Mars was at 22 degrees Sagittarius (travel) trining progressed Uranus, natural ruler of friends, and the progressed eleventh house. Both transiting Mercury (short travels) and transiting Venus (ruler of women) were in Aquarius, which has rulership over friends. And, transiting Venus was exactly conjunct progressed Venus in Aquarius, indicating possibly more than one companion. With both Mercury and transiting Venus in Aquarius, more than one companion was possible. As both Mercury and transiting Venus were in the progressed tenth house, one of the companions had an out of town lecture which the others wanted to attend.

The accident occurred on January 19. The transiting Moon was at 17 degrees Aries squaring progressed Mars at 17 degrees Capricorn; Mars was involved with the Lunation by a previous conjunction in the ninth house. However, transiting Moon at 17 degrees Aries in the natal first house was trining natal Mars at 16 degrees Sagittarius at the same time. That saved the day.

The individual was driving her friend, who was lecturing for an out of town organization, along with another female companion. A tire blew out on an interstate highway (transiting Moon square progressed Mars) on a dismal day with rain mixed with snow, when out of nowhere appeared unexpectedly (Uranus) three men (transiting Mars in Sagittarius - male strangers - trined progressed Uranus on the day of Lunation). These men not only stopped to fix and change the tire, but refused all offers of monetary reward. On one hand, there was an offer of help with no money involved (Mars ruler of the second house of money and trine progressed Uranus), and on the other hand, an unexpected expense for the individual because the tire was irreparable.

The opposition to both natal and progressed Pluto from the Lunation was the delay in getting to the lecture because of the time it took to get the tire changed.

Other features to note the day of the car trouble were transiting Venus and transiting Mercury at 16 degrees Aquarius in the natal twelfth house, exactly sextile natal Mars at 16 degrees Sagittarius in the natal ninth house. This indicated travel with a female friend and companion and the gain of unexpected help (Aquarius) from male strangers (natal Mars in the ninth house of strangers and in Sagittarius). It confirms the aspect of the transiting Moon at 17 degrees Aries, which trined natal Mars at 16 degrees Sagittarius from the first house to the ninth house.

By applying techniques from the book *From One House to An-*

other to this eleventh house (friends and organizations) Lunation, it is clear that the individual's friend was to receive some money for speaking at a club or organization. Venus and Mercury in the natal twelfth house (the second house from the eleventh house of friends) indicates the friend's personal income. Venus rules the natal third house, which is the friend's fifth house of schools, and Mercury rules the native's seventh house, which is the friend's ninth house of colleges and higher education. Transiting Mars at 22 degrees Sagittarius in the natal tenth house was trine progressed Uranus from the tenth house, which is the friend's twelfth house of delays, and Uranus in the first house is the friend's third house of short travels. This trine promised the delay would not cancel the lecture despite some concern on the part of the college organization that the speaker would not be present. Transiting Jupiter was at 15 degrees Pisces in the natal first house (the friend's third house of short travel) and trined transiting Saturn at 15 degrees Cancer. Saturn, ruler of the eleventh house of friends, was another aspect of delays but one that would prove favorable. The moral of this story is don't get upset by heavy aspects on the day of the Lunation without first weighing the favorable aspects. After all, events cannot be exciting every month.

Twelfth House Lunation

This Lunation took place in the natal twelfth house on January 31, 1976 at 10 degrees Aquarius, a sign that usually brings the unexpected. Located in the twelfth house, it could indicate unexpected sorrows and matters to do with hospitals when heavily afflicted as was the case in this chart.

Several deaths and an accident were inevitable before the Full Moon occured. Why the certainty of death in this chart? There is more than one configuration.

In the natal chart, the New Moon squared the natal Sun and transiting Uranus at seven degrees Scorpio, both in a sign that has a natural affinity with death. Their position in the natal eighth house of death does give added emphasis to this indication.

Who died during the succeeding two weeks? Remember, the Lunation indicated a starting point and because it was in the natal twelfth house, this investigation will begin there even though it reveals the second death that occured rather than the first.

The twelfth house is not only hospitals and sorrows, but also governs aunts and uncles (in polarity with the sixth house). The Lunation was conjunct natal Saturn at 9 degrees Aquarius in the natal twelfth house, which leans toward an older person, possibly an aunt or uncle. In the progressed chart the New Moon was conjunct both progressed Venus at 6 degrees Aquarius and Saturn at 12 degrees Aquarius in the progressed tenth house, and Venus is the ruler of the

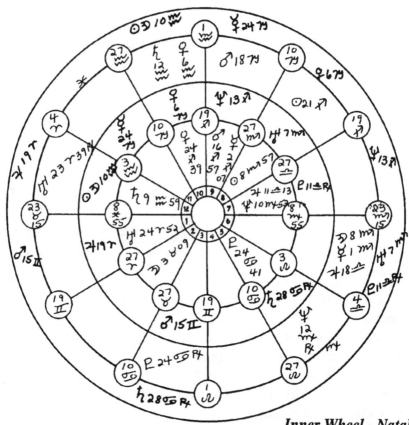

Inner Wheel - Natal
Second Wheel - Transiting
Third Wheel - Progressed
Outer Wheel - Transiting

progressed sixth house of aunts and uncles or co-workers. The New Moon also squared both the progressed Moon at 8 degrees Scorpio and transiting Uranus at 7 degrees Scorpio in the sixth house, endorsing a heavy Scorpio coloring. Progressed Venus in the tenth house squared transiting Uranus at 7 degrees Scorpio and was positioned in the progressed sixth house, a third configuration of sixth house matters.

Another indication of the aunt's death was transiting Mercury at 24 degrees Capricorn in the natal eleventh house (the aunt's twelfth house of hospitals), suggesting an aunt might be in the hospital.

Transiting Mercury opposed natal Pluto in the fifth house (the aunt's sixth house of health) at 24 degrees Cancer and squared natal Uranus at 24 degrees Aries, ruler of the twelfth house of aunts and uncles. Note carefully that Mercury rules the seventh, which is the twelfth house aunt's eighth house of death. This author's book, *From One House To Another*, explains the derivative house system in more detail.

The aunt died five days later on February 5 when the transiting Moon entered the natal first house and was conjunct natal Uranus, ruler of the natal twelfth house of aunts and uncles. Remember, when the Lunation takes place in a certain house, followed by the Moon leaving its conjunction with the Sun and making an aspect to the ruler of the house in which the Lunation took place, it often sets off the action promised by the New Moon.

The first death occurred on the day of the Lunation when a boss of the native died suddenly of a heart attack. The New Moon at 10 degrees Aquarius squared the natal Sun at 8 degrees Scorpio. Transiting Uranus was conjunct the Sun at 7 degrees Scorpio, indicating something unexpected would happen to a male boss, possibly a heart attack (Sun).

Why a boss? It was stated in the introduction that transiting planets around the natal or progressed chart act like a mini-scope on the days of the New and Full Moons. Transiting Venus, ruler of the eighth house of death was in the natal tenth house and also in Capricorn, two of the boss' configurations. Looking at the fifth house, which is the boss' eighth house of death, there is transiting Saturn, natural ruler of bosses. In addition, natal Pluto was opposed by transiting Mercury at 24 degrees Capricorn, a sign that governs bosses.

In the progressed chart the New Moon took place in the progressed tenth house of bosses conjunct progressed Saturn at 12 degrees Aquarius, which is the ruler of the ninth house (the boss' twelfth house of hospitals).

He died of a heart attack when the transiting Moon left the conjunction of the Sun and was conjunct progressed Saturn (natural ruler of bosses) at 12 degrees Aquarius, a sign that rules the unexpected and confirms the Sun/Uranus conjunction in the eighth house and Scorpio.

Transiting Mercury was also in the progressed ninth house opposing progressed Pluto at 24 degrees Cancer retrograde in the progressed third house. Mercury also squared progressed Uranus at 23 degrees Aries retrograde in the twelfth house, which is the boss' third house of accidents. This indicated a possible accident involving still another executive or boss in this native's department of work.

Transiting Jupiter at 19 degrees Aries in the progressed twelfth house opposed progressed Jupiter at 18 degrees Libra in the progressed sixth house, and both Jupiters were in a T-square with progressed Mars at 18 degrees Capricorn in the progressed ninth house. Both Jupiters were rulers of the progressed eighth house of insurance and of course Mars in Capricorn added fuel to the fire for it is also representative of superiors.

On February 2, 1976, the transiting Moon entered Pisces (hospitals) and squared the natal Mars at 16 degrees Sagittarius in the natal ninth house, which is the boss' twelfth house of hospitals. This superior had a serious accident. With both Jupiters squaring Mars on the day of the New Moon his car was demolished, although he was not seriously injured except for the neck (the Lunation was conjunct Venus in Aquarius and Venus rules the throat and neck area) and had to wear a brace because of whiplash.

However, he did not fare too well financially through the insurance company as the chart will disclose. Both transiting and progressed Jupiter, ruler of the progressed eighth house, squared progressed Mars.

Transiting Mercury was positioned in the natal eleventh house (the boss' second house of money) and opposed natal Pluto (natural ruler of insurance) in the fifth house (the boss's eighth house of insurance and money belonging to others), confirming the Jupiter and Mars aspect. Transiting Mercury also squared natal Uranus, ruler of the natal twelfth house, which is the boss' third house of accidents. There would be an unexpected accident resulting in financial problems because the insurance company would not see eye to eye on the settlement of his car.

As is evident, the natal chart stressed more the death of the aunt with the Lunation in natal twelfth, while the progressed chart clearly stated other individuals, such as bosses, since the New Moon was positioned in the progressed tenth house.

Twelfth
House Lunation

This Lunation took place on March 30, 1976 in the native's natal twelfth house at 9 degrees Aries. The New Moon was conjunct transiting Mercury at 9 degrees Aries and natal Mars at 5 degrees Aries as well as trine natal Venus at 9 degrees Leo in the fifth house of children. There was a possibility that a child, perhaps a female child (Venus in Leo in the fifth house) would need surgery (Lunation conjunct natal Mars, ruler of surgery). However, because of the trine to Venus, the surgery might be beneficial to the child.

As it turned out, the child needed corrective surgery for a hearing problem (Lunation conjunct transiting Mercury which rules the sense of hearing). The operation was a success.

Glancing at the rest of the transiting planets, note that they did not make any close aspects to natal or progressed planets, except for transiting Mars in the natal third house of brothers and sisters squaring natal Mars in the twelfth house of hospitals.

An older sister (Mars in Cancer) also needed minor surgery. Except for these two incidents, the rest of the month was rather quiet.

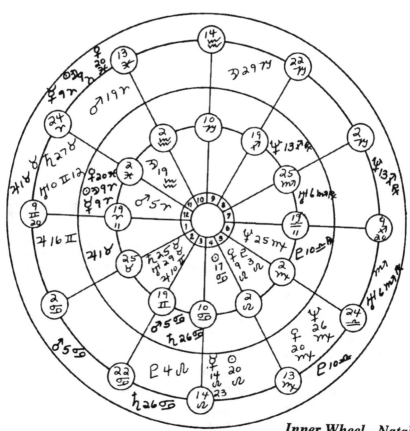

Inner Wheel - Natal
Second Wheel - Transiting
Third Wheel - Progressed
Outer Wheel - Transiting

Tenth House
New Moon

The New Moon took place in the natal tenth house at 8 degrees Gemini. A double sign in the house of career could only mean one thing: a possibility of two job offers.

The native did receive two job offers to sing in nightclubs. One was at a local nightclub, however the other offer fell through. The Lunation squared natal Venus at 11 degrees Pisces in the seventh house of partnerships with Venus as ruler of the tenth house of career. The other employer wanted one person rather than a duet and her partner was accepted in place of her.

However, in the progressed chart transiting Venus at 2 degrees Gemini was conjunct her progressed Sun at 3 degrees Gemini and sextile her natal Mars at 3 degrees Leo. With the Sun ruling her natal Ascendant and Venus ruling her second house of money, the second job offer was terrific. Another interesting occurrence that happened during the ensuing month was a mix-up with her medical prescription.

Transiting Venus was conjunct her progressed Sun at 3 degrees Gemini and both planets were square progressed Neptune (natural ruler of drugs and medication and of the progressed sixth) at 3 degrees Virgo (matters to do with health) in the progressed twelfth house of confusion. However, transiting Uranus at 3 degrees Scorpio in the natal third house was sextile natal Neptune in Virgo, so the mix-up was not of a serious consequence. The Sun is a male influence and

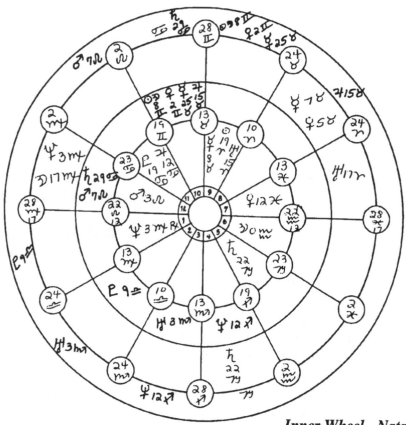

Inner Wheel - Natal
Second Wheel - Transiting
Third Wheel - Progressed
Outer Wheel - Transiting

in the sign Gemini there would be communication or some kind of written matter to do with a male, and confusion or a mix-up with drugs and prescriptions (Neptune) that was necessary for one's health (Neptune in Virgo). The pharmacist gave her a prescription written for another patient by the same doctor. Because she had been fore-warned of this possible condition, she immediately recognized that it was the wrong one and a glance at the bottle indicated the difference in the patient's name.

The situation could have been dangerous had she taken the pills and perhaps received ill effects from them. The confusion did not end here, for when she returned the prescription the pharmacist made another error in the count and gave her only half the amount of pills the prescription called for even though she had paid for the full amount (Lunation conjunct transiting Venus, ruler of the natal second and square progressed and natal Neptune). She had to return again and try to straighten out the situation.

During the ensuing month she also met an interesting gentleman. He was a Gemini (transiting Venus in Gemini conjunct the progressed Sun, ruler of the progressed eleventh house), however because the Lunation squared her natal Venus at 11 degrees Pisces, she was cautioned that there was something hidden about his background because Venus and the progressed Sun also squared her natal Neptune. It turned out that he was married and only interested in a sexual affair, (Neptune rules the natal eighth house - a clandestine, sexual encounter).

Eighth House
Solar Eclipse

Chart A is a man's natal chart for a kidney transplant which took place November 12, 1992. Any time one's health appears to be in jeopardy there will always be an aspect linking the two rulers of the sixth house cusps, one natal and the other progressed. This man has progressed Mercury at 23 degrees Scorpio in semi-square aspect with progressed Venus at 8 degrees Libra. Venus is the ruler of the natal sixth house cusp and Mercury is the ruler of the progressed sixth house cusp (see progressed Chart B).

The slow planets do not progress as rapidly as the Moon, Sun, Mercury, Venus and Mars and thus are less likely to form aspects between themselves. Therefore, when the sign Scorpio, Sagittarius, Capricorn, Aquarius or Pisces is on the natal house cusp, use the "transiting" ruler of the natal house cusp in aspect to the planet that rules the progressed house cusp. For example, if Scorpio is on the natal sixth house cusp and by progression Sagittarius is on the progressed sixth house cusp, it will be necessary to rely on transiting Pluto to aspect either natal or progressed Jupiter (ruler of the progressed sixth house cusp), or transiting Jupiter in aspect with natal or progressed Pluto. It does not always indicate a health problem; with soft aspects one can expect positive job changes.

One should always take note when both Solar and Lunar Eclipses highlight natal and progressed planets. In natal Chart A, the previous Solar Eclipse of June 30, 1992 at 8 degrees Cancer took place in the

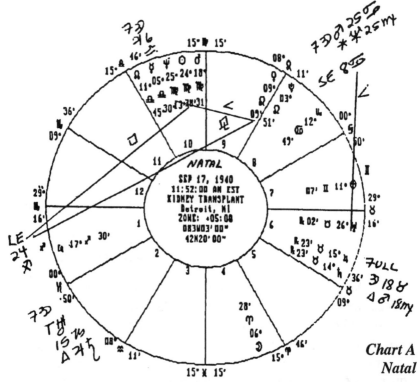

Chart A
Natal

natal eighth house of surgery and made a semisquare aspect to natal Uranus at 26 degrees Taurus in the natal sixth house. Natal Venus, ruler of the natal sixth house cusp, received a sesquisquare aspect from the Lunar Eclipse of June 15, 1992 at 24 degrees Sagittarius, which fell in the natal first house.

The Lunar Eclipse at 24 degrees Sagittarius also made an exact square to the natal Sun, ruler of the ninth house cusp. Natal Venus is in the natal ninth house in semisquare aspect with natal Sun at 24 degrees Virgo. The only large hospital capable of handling a kidney transplant was 90 miles from where he lived (Venus in the ninth house semisquare the ruler of the ninth house cusp with both receiving a hard aspect from a Lunar Eclipse in the twelfth house of hospitals).

Progressed Chart B has the Solar Eclipse of June 30, 1992 at 8 degrees Cancer in the natal sixth house exactly square progressed Venus at 8 Degrees Libra in the progressed ninth house, which in turn was in a progressed semisquare aspect with progressed Mercury, ruler of the progressed sixth house cusp. Venus is ruler of the natal

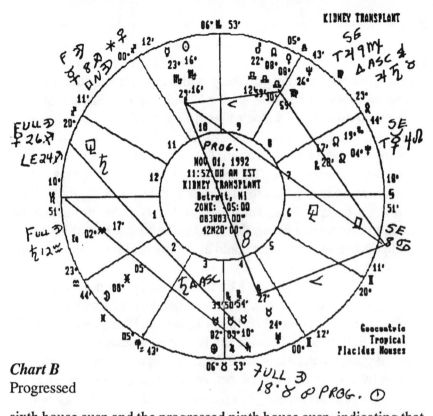

Chart B
Progressed

sixth house cusp and the progressed ninth house cusp, indicating that a health matter might require medical treatment at a distance.

Surgery was confirmed through transiting Mercury, ruler of the progressed sixth house cusp at 4 degrees Leo (at the time of the Solar Eclipse) and exactly conjunct progressed Pluto (ruler of the natal Scorpio Ascendant). The ruler of the progressed sixth house was conjunct the ruler of the natal Ascendant, offering another confirmation of first/sixth house involvement.

The required hospital stay at a distance was confirmed when the Lunar Eclipse of June 15, 1992 at 24 degrees Sagittarius (natural ruler of distant places) occurred in the progressed twelfth house of hospitals and sesquisquared progressed Saturn (ruler of the progressed Ascendant) in the progressed fourth house. That, along with the Mercury/Pluto conjunction, provided an additional clue that the native would be personally involved (twelfth house Lunar Eclipse sesquisquare natal Saturn, ruler of the progressed Ascendant).

However there was one very good saving grace as progressed

Saturn, ruler of the progressed Ascendant, was at 10 degrees Taurus in an exact trine to the progressed Ascendant's degree. Whatever pain or discomfort he had to endure through the difficult kidney transplant would all be worthwhile with the promise of complete success.

The progressed chart was set for November 1, 1992; at that time it was unknown that a kidney would be available. The progressed Moon was at 8 degrees Pisces in the progressed second house, indicating that the hospitalization (Pisces) insurance might not cover all the medical expenses. The progressed Moon at 8 degrees Pisces made an exact inconjunct to progressed Venus at 8 degrees Libra, requiring a major adjustment to a new lifestyle due to medication (Moon in Pisces) that he would have to take for the rest of his life to avoid possible rejection that could affect his health (Venus rules his natal sixth house cusp).

The kidney transplant was a complete success as indicated by the Full Moon prior to the surgery. Refer to natal Chart A and notice that the Full Moon of November 10, 1992 was at 18 degrees Taurus in his natal sixth house of health and it formed an exact trine with the surgical planet, natal Mars at 18 degrees Virgo. When there are two aspects involving the same planet, one natal and the other a transit, and if both are soft aspects, it is a clear cut indication that all will go well. Not only was natal Mars receiving an exact trine from the Full Moon, but transiting Mars at 25 degrees Cancer was in the eighth house of surgery in an exact sextile with natal Neptune at 25 degrees Virgo (the planet that governs substitutes and transplants) and natal Neptune rules his fourth house (end of the matter).

Transiting Jupiter on the day of the Full Moon (ruler of the progressed twelfth house cusp) was at 6 degrees Libra within one degree of conjunction with natal Mercury, ruler of the progressed sixth house cusp. This offered additional luck and protection.

In the progressed Chart B, the Full Moon of November 10, 1992 was at 18 degrees Taurus in the progressed fourth house in close opposition to the progressed Sun at 16 degrees Scorpio, ruler of the progressed eighth house of surgery. Any time a New or Full Moon is higher in degree than a natal or progressed planet it is aspecting, it is an indication of something from the past already put into motion that may have to be handled in the next few weeks. He had been patiently waiting for a kidney donor and the Full Moon finally brought the matter to a head.

Transiting Mercury at the time of the Full Moon was at 8 degrees Sagittarius in exact sextile with progressed Venus. Mercury, ruler of the progressed sixth house cusp in Sagittarius also confirmed an unexpected (Mercury in the eleventh house) opportunity would arise involving health issues (Mercury rules the progressed sixth house cusp and Venus rules the natal sixth house cusp). Transiting Mercury's position in Sagittarius (distance) and in sextile with progressed Venus in the ninth house (also ruler of the progressed ninth house cusp) provided additional insight that he would have to travel to a hospital in a city 90 miles away.

Even transiting Jupiter on the day of the Solar Eclipse confirmed that surgery would be performed at a distant hospital. Notice that transiting Jupiter at the time of the Solar Eclipse was at 9 degrees Virgo in the eighth house of surgery in trine aspect with the progressed Ascendant, progressed Jupiter and Saturn, ruler of the progressed Ascendant. Transiting Jupiter in Virgo (a medical center in a distant city) was trining progressed Jupiter in the fourth house (end of the matter), and Jupiter rules the progressed twelfth house of hospitals with Sagittarius on the house cusp.

Individuals who have Sagittarius on their natal or progressed twelfth house cusp or planets in the twelfth house in Sagittarius may, at some point in life, have to enter a larger than average hospital. But this placement has to be confirmed through planets in the natal or progressed ninth house or their rulers.

The fact that he would be required to take medication for the rest of his life to avoid possible rejection of the kidney transplant is confirmed with transiting Venus at 26 degrees Sagittarius (at the time of the Full Moon) in an exact square with progressed Neptune at 26 degrees Virgo in the progressed eighth house of surgery. Additional confirmation is derived from transiting Mercury at 8 degrees Sagittarius (at the time of the Full Moon) in an exact square with progressed Moon at 8 degrees Pisces (twelfth house, Neptune and Pisces govern the necessary requirement for life saving medication). This is especially true with transiting Venus and Mercury simultaneously aspecting planets in Pisces or Neptune (natural ruler of medication). And most important is having both Mercury and Venus as rulers of the natal and progressed sixth house cusps.

First House
Solar Eclipse

Mark is one of this author's brilliant students in the advanced adult class at Valley Forge High School. He and his friend were taking a mini weekend vacation trip to Canada but from the looks of her natal and progressed charts, he was concerned that she might become seriously ill. In class I told him I didn't think she would become sick until their return home and to be sure to take her to the hospital at the first sign of illness. He did and was credited by the hospital staff for saving her life due to his quick action.

Mark's friend suffered a brain hemorrhage on October 6, 1990, which attacked the optic nerve and left her blind in her left eye. She was in a coma for several weeks, paralyzed on her left side. Later, she was transferred to a rehabilitation center for 18 months of extensive therapy. When it became apparent she would never again be self sufficient, her parents decided to take her to their home in Florida. Mark was devastated at the thought of losing the woman he loved and planned to marry, but he had no legal right to keep her in Cleveland and take care of her.

There was a Solar Eclipse on July 22, 1990 at 29 degrees Cancer, which occurred in the first house and made a sesquisquare aspect to natal Moon, ruler of the natal Ascendant. It is important to note when an Eclipse falls in one's first house, but it is most important if it also aspects the ruler of the first house cusp.

Transiting Venus on the day of the Solar Eclipse was at 3 degrees

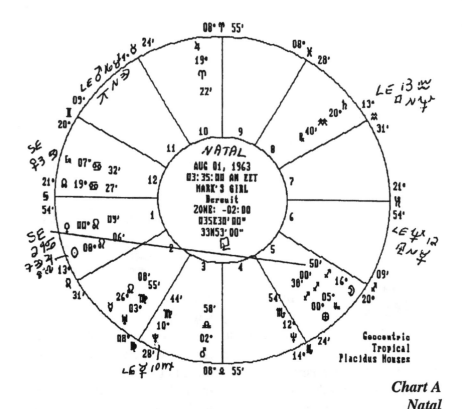

Chart A
Natal

Cancer (ruler of the progressed third house cusp), squaring natal Mars at 3 degrees Aries in the natal third house.

The Lunar Eclipse of August 6, 1990 was at 13 degrees Aquarius in the natal eighth house of surgery square natal Neptune at 12 degrees Scorpio in the natal fourth house. Transiting Neptune was at 12 degrees Capricorn on the day of the Lunar Eclipse in a sesquisquare aspect with natal Mercury at 26 degrees Leo. Mercury rules the natal third of the mind and mental attributes. Transiting Mercury was at 10 degrees Virgo exactly conjunct natal Pluto in the natal third house, indicating possible surgery (Pluto) on the brain (Mercury ruler of the third house cusp conjunct Pluto). She had surgery on her head to relieve the build-up of fluid to avoid further brain damage.

Notice that the Solar Eclipse of July 22, 1990 at 29 degrees Cancer falls in the progressed twelfth house of hospitals and makes the same sesquisquare aspect, but this time to the progressed Moon. Both natal and progressed Moon, ruler of the natal Ascendant, received a hard

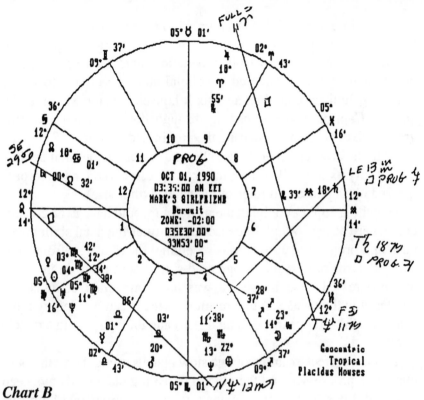

Chart B
Progressed

aspect from the previous Solar Eclipse.

Twelve degrees Leo was on the progressed Ascendant and natal Neptune at 12 degrees Scorpio squared it.

The Lunar Eclipse of August 6, 1990 at 13 degrees Aquarius squared the progressed Neptune at 13 degrees Scorpio and opposed the progressed Ascendant. She had two hard aspects, one to natal Neptune and the other to progressed Neptune. They both rule the natal eighth house cusp.

The Full Moon of October 4, 1990 occurred at 11 degrees Aries, exactly square transiting Neptune at 11 degrees Capricorn in the natal fifth house and progressed sixth house. There were three aspects to one planetary figure: natal Neptune squared the progressed Ascendant, the Solar Eclipse squared progressed Neptune and transiting Neptune received an exact hard aspect from the Full Moon. All indicated she would be confined in a large institution in a distant city (natal Neptune rules the natal ninth house cusp).

At the time of the Full Moon, transiting Jupiter was at 8 degrees Leo, exactly conjunct the natal Sun in the first house at 8 degrees Leo. Ordinarily, a conjunction from a benefic planet such as Jupiter to one's natal Sun is considered beneficial and protective. However, transiting Jupiter rules the natal sixth house cusp and Saturn at 18 degrees Capricorn was transiting through both the natal and progressed sixth house and squaring the progressed Jupiter at 18 degrees Aries in the progressed ninth (another indication of confinement in a distant city as a result of an illness; progressed Jupiter in the progressed ninth house and ruler of the natal sixth house).

Transiting Jupiter conjunct the natal Sun would have to be considered a hard aspect. Why? Because Jupiter rules the natal sixth house cusp and progressed Jupiter was receiving a hard aspect from transiting Saturn (ruler of the progressed sixth house cusp) in the natal and progressed sixth houses. It was the conjunction of transiting Jupiter with the natal Sun that resulted in the loss of her left eye (the Sun rules the left eye in a female's chart and the right eye in a male's chart).

This is a perfect example of two slow planets ruling the sixth house cusp, one progressed and the other a transiting planet. Always keep a watchful eye on two slow planetary configurations that both rule the same house cusp (one natal and the other progressed).

She suffered the brain hemorrhage on October 6, 1992, two days after the Full Moon. Transiting Moon (ruler of the natal Ascendant) reached 13 degrees Taurus in the progressed tenth house, squared the Lunar Eclipse at 13 degrees Aquarius, opposed progressed Neptune at 13 Scorpio and squared the progressed Ascendant at 12 degrees Leo.